GUIDED JOURNAL

GOD *of the* IMPOSSIBLE

Copyright © 2023 by Marsha Smith

Published by Kudu Publishing

All rights reserved. No portion of this book may be reproduced, stored in a retrieval system, or transmitted in any form or by any means—electronic, mechanical, photocopy, recording, scanning, or other—except for brief quotations in critical reviews or articles, without prior written permission of the author.
Scripture quotations marked AMP are taken from the Amplified® Bible (AMP), Copyright © 2015 by The Lockman Foundation. Used by permission. www.lockman.org | Scripture quotations marked ASV are from the American Standard Version of the Holy Bible and are in the public domain. | Scripture quotations marked BLB are taken from The Holy Bible, Berean Literal Bible, BLB. Copyright ©2016, 2018 by Bible Hub. Used by Permission. All Rights Reserved Worldwide. www.berean.bible |Scripture quotations marked BSB are from The Holy Bible, Berean Study Bible, BSB, Copyright ©2016, 2020 by Bible Hub Used by Permission. All Rights Reserved Worldwide. | Scripture quotations marked CSB have been taken from the Christian Standard Bible®, Copyright © 2017 by Holman Bible Publishers. Used by permission. Christian Standard Bible® and CSB® are federally registered trademarks of Holman Bible Publishers. | Scripture quotations marked ESV are from The ESV® Bible (The Holy Bible, English Standard Version®), copyright © 2001 by Crossway, a publishing ministry of Good News Publishers. Used by permission. All rights reserved. | Scripture quotations marked HCSB are taken from the Holman Christian Standard Bible®, Used by Permission HCSB ©1999, 2000, 2002, 2003, 2009 Holman Bible Publishers. Holman Christian Standard Bible®, Holman CSB®, and HCSB® are federally registered trademarks of Holman Bible Publishers. | Scripture quotations marked KJV are taken from the King James Version of the Bible. Public domain. | Scripture quotations marked LSB are taken from the (LSB®) Legacy Standard Bible®, Copyright © 2021 by The Lockman Foundation. Used by permission. All rights reserved. Managed in partnership with Three Sixteen Publishing Inc. LSBible.org and 316publishing.com. | Scripture quotations marked MSG are taken from THE MESSAGE, copyright © 1993, 1994, 1995, 1996, 2000, 2001, 2002 by Eugene H. Peterson. Used by permission of NavPress. All rights reserved. Represented by Tyndale House Publishers, Inc. | Scripture quotations marked NASB are taken from the (NASB®) New American Standard Bible®, Copyright © 1960, 1971, 1977, 1995, 2020 by The Lockman Foundation. Used by permission. All rights reserved. www.lockman.org | Scripture quotations marked NIV are taken from the Holy Bible, New International Version®, NIV®. Copyright © 1973, 1978, 1984, 2011 by Biblica, Inc.™ Used by permission of Zondervan. All rights reserved worldwide. www.zondervan.com. The "NIV" and "New International Version" are trademarks registered in the United States Patent and Trademark Office by Biblica, Inc.™ | Scripture quotations marked NKJV are taken from the New King James Version®. Copyright © 1982 by Thomas Nelson. Used by permission. All rights reserved. | Scripture quotations marked NLT are taken from the Holy Bible, New Living Translation, copyright © 1996, 2004, 2015 by Tyndale House Foundation. Used by permission of Tyndale House Publishers, Inc., Carol Stream, Illinois 60188. All rights reserved.

For foreign and subsidiary rights, contact the author.

Cover design by: Sara Young
Cover photo by: Kiki Smith Photography

ISBN: 978-1-962401-05-0   1 2 3 4 5 6 7 8 9 10

Printed in the United States of America

MARSHA SMITH, MD, FAAN

The exceedingly abundant life in spite of detours!

GOD *of the* IMPOSSIBLE

GUIDED JOURNAL

Contents

CHAPTER 1. *The Battle in the Wilderness* 7

CHAPTER 2. *The Lord Giveth and Taketh Away* 17

CHAPTER 3. *Discerning God's Voice in the Detours* 27

CHAPTER 4. *Accepting God's Will* 37

CHAPTER 5. *Overcoming Hardships* 47

CHAPTER 6. *Lessons in Grief and Pain (Nothing is Wasted)* . . .57

CHAPTER 7. *Endurance Through the Race of Life* 69

CHAPTER 1

The Battle in the Wilderness

> *"When the righteous cry for help, the Lord hears and delivers them out of all their troubles."*
> —Psalm 34:17 (ESV)

Sometimes, life takes an unexpected turn for the worst—our lives are shattered, turned upside down, our plans thwarted. We try to make sense of it but find ourselves spinning out, unable to see how God's plan for our lives could include something so tragic and agonizing. Maybe you've experienced a significant loss, received a harrowing medical report, or lost a job. Our wilderness seasons take on many different shapes and sizes, but they all have one thing in common: they rock us to the core. Fortunately, the grace of God turns our graveyards into flourishing gardens. He never retreats.

> MY GRANDMOTHER WAS ONE OF THE STRONGEST CHRISTIAN WOMEN I EVER KNEW AND TAUGHT US TO HAVE A FEAR AND A REVERENCE FOR GOD THAT WOULD LAST MY ENTIRE LIFE. SHE HAD A FAITH IN GOD THAT NEVER WAVERED, DESPITE LIFE'S MANY STORMS.

Questions to Consider

As you read Chapter 1: "The Battle in the Wilderness" in *God of the Impossible,* reflect on these questions, wrestle with them, and give yourself room to generate more questions as you journal. Take your time with each one—approach them with intention and patience. Ask the Holy Spirit to reveal His heart to you, as He brings to your remembrance all that is needed to usher in healing for your heart.

What is your wilderness story? What happened to you that changed the course of your life forever? How did you respond to this event?

_____
_____
_____
_____
_____
_____
_____

Guided Journal

How did your upbringing impact how you navigated your wilderness season? Did it serve you? Did it hinder your healing? In what ways?

_____
_____
_____
_____
_____
_____

How did your relationship with God evolve throughout the pain, uncertainty, and unanswered questions?

_____
_____
_____
_____
_____
_____
_____

> **IT WAS A REAL TEST OF MY TRUST AND FAITH IN GOD AND WHAT I TRULY BELIEVE WAS HIS PURPOSE FOR MY LIFE THAT I CONTINUED IN SCHOOL AND DIDN'T LISTEN TO WHAT THE DOCTOR HAD TO SAY TO ME ABOUT SWITCHING CAREERS.**

In what ways has hardship drawn you closer to God's purpose for your life? What do you see now that you didn't see before? Are you still seeking closure or answers?

_____
_____
_____
_____
_____

What have you noticed about God as you have journeyed through your wilderness seasons? What have you learned about Him? If you have had difficulty seeing His hand in the middle of the mess, can you see it now, and in what ways?

_____
_____
_____
_____
_____

What kind of social support did you have during this time (family, friends, pastors)? What did your healing journey look like if you didn't have proper social support? How did God provide for you to accommodate your needs?

_____
_____

Consider these Scriptures and answer the following questions:

"For thou hast possessed my reins: thou hast covered me in my mother's womb. I will praise thee; for I am fearfully and wonderfully made: marvelous are they works; and that my soul knoweth right well."
—Psalm 139:13-14 (KJV)

Why is this Scripture meaningful for finding rest in times of grief and loss?

___

Sometimes, grief can cause us to question whether we are loved, seen, and heard by the One who formed us. What does this verse reveal about your identity in Him?

___

What do you think David meant when he acknowledged that his soul knows of God's works as marvelous?

Do you believe that God uses your pain for your good and God's glory? In what ways have you questioned this in the past? What kind of questions do you wrestle with now?

Guided Journal

"The effectual fervent prayers of a righteous man availeth much."
—James 5:16 (KJV)

What does this Scripture mean in light of persevering through grief?

_____
_____
_____
_____
_____
_____
_____
_____

When and where have you seen answered prayer in your life? How did He answer it and what does that tell you about His character when all seems lost?

_____
_____
_____
_____
_____
_____
_____
_____

Write Your Own Prayer

On the lines below, craft your own personal prayer to the Lord. Draw from your answers above as inspiration for the requests you have for God. Ask Him for intimate guidance on what is most important to Him for your healing as you navigate through your own wilderness.

_____

_____

_____

_____

_____

_____

_____

_____

_____

_____

_____

_____

_____

_____

_____

_____

_____

_____

_____

_____

Guided Journal

Noted Scriptures

On the lines below, write down a few encouraging Scriptures that you can meditate on, commit to memory, and recite as an expression of hopeful expectation to see God's promises come to pass in your life.

CHAPTER 2

The Lord Giveth and Taketh Away

> *"God is faithful, through whom ye were called into the fellowship of his Son Jesus Christ our Lord."*
> —1 Corinthians 1:9 (ASV)

As Christians, we often associate the word "blessings" from God with gifts that make us happy. The truth is—sometimes to our dismay—blessings are often disguised as curses because of the pain and suffering they induce. As we allow loss to mature us in Christ, we give God room to do the miraculous within us and through us. True worship is not reserved only for the mountaintops. In fact, the power of our lives in Christ is found in the devotion of our hearts when we are stuck in the valleys.

I CAN CHOOSE TO SEE THE "IAM" IN EVERY SITUATION.

Questions to Consider

As you read Chapter 2: "The Lord Giveth and Taketh Away" in *God of the Impossible*, reflect on these questions, wrestle with them, and give yourself room to develop more questions as you journal. Take your time with each one—approach them with intention and patience. Ask the Holy Spirit to reveal His heart to you, as He brings to your remembrance all that is needed to usher in healing for your heart.

Have you ever thought things couldn't get worse . . . until they did? Describe the experience and how it made you feel.

_____
_____
_____
_____
_____
_____
_____

Why do you think God sometimes allows the bottom to fall out of our lives? What is your reaction to that?

_____
_____
_____
_____
_____
_____

What kind of conversations have you had with God in moments of desperation and heartache? What have you learned about prayer during suffering?

___

> ## I DIDN'T PRAY FOR SEVERAL MONTHS BECAUSE I WAS SO BLINDED BY THE RAGE AND ANGER I DIRECTED AT GOD.

___

Have you or anyone else you've known been impacted by depression and/or suicide? Who did you run to for rescue?

Where have you seen God's faithfulness in the midst of depression, or are you still trying to find it? Do you know someone who is? What would you say to them to comfort them?

_____
_____
_____
_____
_____
_____

Describe the story of a time when God delivered you from depression and/or suicidal thoughts. What do you remember about this story that revealed a dimension of Him you had not yet seen?

_____
_____
_____
_____
_____
_____

Think of a time when you have been angry with God. In what ways did that anger hinder your healing? Did it serve you in any way? When did you notice your anger began to dissipate, and why do you think that is?

_____
_____
_____
_____

Consider these Scriptures and answer the following questions:

But let all who take refuge in You rejoice; let them sing joyful praises forever. Spread your protection over them, that all who love Your name be filled with joy. For You bless the godly, O Lord; You surround them with Your shield of love.
—Psalm 5:11-12 (NLT)

Have you ever found it difficult to praise God through life's storms? Can you think of a time when you pushed through that resistance and praised Him anyway? What did that do for your spirit?

How does the enemy tempt you into doubting God's faithfulness and care for you? Do you take the bait? Explain how the enemy's role in your life has changed over the past 5 years.

_____

_____

_____

_____

_____

_____

Do you know anyone who praises God with reckless abandon? Who in your life encourages you to worship without cause?

_____

_____

_____

_____

_____

_____

_____

His wife said to him, "Are you still trying to maintain your integrity? Curse God and die!" But Job replied, "You talk like a foolish woman. Should we accept only good things from the hand of God and never anything bad?"
—Job 2:9-10(NLT)

What kind of thoughts and emotions come up for you as you read this Scripture from Job? In what ways does your conception of a life laid down for God mimic that of Job's? In what ways does it oppose it?

_____
_____
_____
_____
_____
_____
_____

What does it mean to "accept" bad things from the hand of God? Does this change your view of God in any way? Explain. What kind of fruit comes from accepting unpleasant or unwanted outcomes in our lives?

_____
_____
_____
_____
_____
_____
_____
_____

Write Your Own Prayer

On the lines below, craft your own personal prayer to the Lord. Draw from your answers above as inspiration for the requests you have for God. Ask Him for intimate guidance on what is most important to Him for helping you resist the devil and praise Him anyway.

_____
_____
_____
_____
_____
_____
_____
_____
_____
_____
_____
_____
_____
_____
_____
_____
_____
_____
_____
_____

Guided Journal

Noted Scriptures

On the lines below, write down a few encouraging Scriptures that you can meditate on, commit to memory, and recite as an expression of hopeful expectation to see God's promises come to pass in your life.

_____
_____
_____
_____
_____
_____
_____
_____
_____
_____
_____
_____
_____
_____
_____
_____
_____
_____
_____
_____

CHAPTER 3

Discerning God's Voice in the Detours

"The Lord your God is in your midst, A victorious warrior. He will exult over you with joy, He will be quiet in His love, He will rejoice over you with shouts of joy."
—Zephaniah 3:17 (NASB)

||||||||||||||||||||||||||||||||||||||||||||||||||||||

Hearing the voice of God is the key to putting one foot in front of the other as we travail through the aftermath of grief and loss. Sometimes, grief's knock on our door can be deafening; it can stifle and even smother God's gentle whispers. Fortunately, God has a way of unclogging our ears, because speaking to His children is His greatest delight.

||||||||||||||||||||||||||||||||||||||||||||||||||||||||||||||||||||||||||||||||||

WE CAN TURN UP THE VOLUME OF GOD'S WORD SO THAT WE CAN WITHSTAND THE DARTS OF THE ENEMY AND TUNE OUT HIS LIES AND DECEPTION.

||||||||||||||||||||||||||||||||||||||||||||||||||||||||||||||||||||||||||||||||||

Questions to Consider

As you read Chapter 3: "Discerning God's Voice in the Detours" in *God of the Impossible*, reflect on these questions, wrestle with them, and give yourself room to develop more questions as you journal. Take your time with each one—approach them with intention and patience. Ask the Holy Spirit to reveal His heart to you, as He brings to your remembrance all that is needed to usher in healing for your heart.

Do you ever feel like your inner GPS is off? Do you ever feel like it is re-routing you in a direction you don't want to go? Provide a personal example.

_____
_____
_____
_____
_____
_____
_____

Guided Journal

To what degree are you in tune with your spiritual GPS?

___

How do you know when you are following the voice of God? Have you ever felt confused about whether you are hearing God's voice, your own voice, or even the enemy's voice? Why?

___

How would your life change if you could hear the voice of God and follow His will for your life with total clarity? What could you do today to begin calibrating your GPS?

___

WE MUST ALLOW THE HOLY SPIRIT TO REVEAL THE HINDRANCE AND TO HELP US TURN AWAY FROM IT SO THAT DISCERNING CAN BECOME MUCH EASIER FOR US.

Why is it so important to follow the voice of God? Think of a time when you turned the volume down on God's voice and turned the volume of the enemy's voice up. What transpired?

_____
_____
_____
_____
_____

What do you think hinders you from hearing the voice of God? What hinders you from obeying the voice of God?

_____
_____
_____
_____
_____

In what ways has obedience to God's voice ushered healing into your life? In what ways has disobedience to His voice hindered healing?

_____
_____
_____
_____
_____

Consider these Scriptures and answer the following questions:

"For God is not a God of confusion but of peace."
—1 Corinthians 14:33 (ESV)

How has this Scripture applied to your life, either in the present or in the past?

_____
_____
_____
_____

Think about an upheaval in your life that hindered your ability to hear the voice of God. What did you make of that confusion?

_____
_____
_____
_____
_____

What kind of confusion are you experiencing now and why? What have you or are you learning?

_____
_____
_____
_____

GOD *of the* IMPOSSIBLE

"I will instruct you and teach you in the way which you should go; I will counsel you with My eye upon you."
—Psalm 32:8 (NASB)

What does this Scripture say about God as your protector?

_____
_____
_____
_____
_____
_____
_____

What has God taught you about grief and loss that you didn't understand before? How has your perspective changed?

_____
_____
_____
_____
_____
_____
_____
_____
_____

What steps could you take to allow His instruction to change your heart around grief and loss?

___

How does it make you feel to know that God has His eye upon you? Can you believe it, even if you don't feel it?

___

Do you expect to hear God's voice? Why or why not?

___

Write Your Own Prayer

On the lines below, craft your own personal prayer to the Lord. Draw from your answers above as inspiration for the requests you have for God. Ask Him for intimate guidance on what is most important to Him to help you hear His voice and clear any confusion that is keeping you from His perfect will.

_____

_____

_____

_____

_____

_____

_____

_____

_____

_____

_____

_____

_____

_____

_____

_____

_____

_____

_____

Noted Scriptures

On the lines below, write down a few encouraging Scriptures that you can meditate on, commit to memory, and recite as an expression of hopeful expectation to see God's promises come to pass in your life.

_____
_____
_____
_____
_____
_____
_____
_____
_____
_____
_____
_____
_____
_____
_____
_____
_____
_____
_____
_____
_____
_____
_____
_____

CHAPTER 4

Accepting God's Will

"I cry out to God Most High, to God who fulfills His purpose for me."
—Psalm 57:2 (BSB)

||||||||||||||||||||||||||||||||||||||||||||||||||||

God has written a story that is uniquely fitted for each one of us. Our walks bear witness to the multi-dimensional God that we serve. But each unique story carries a familiar scene—the path that did not look like the one we paved in our minds. Even more, we have to learn how to walk that path free of bitterness, resentment, and anger toward God, because our feelings are lousy gauges of the best that God has in store for us all.

||||||||||||||||||||||||||||||||||||||||||||||||||||||||||||||

PART OF ACCEPTING GOD'S WILL IS LAYING DOWN OUR RIGHTS AND OUR DESIRES AND PICKING UP HIS WILL AND TRUSTING WHAT GOD IS DOING.

||||||||||||||||||||||||||||||||||||||||||||||||||||||||||||||

Questions to Consider:

As you read Chapter 4: "Accepting God's Will" in *God of the Impossible*, reflect on these questions, wrestle with them, and give yourself room to develop more questions as you journal. Take your time with each one—approach them with intention and patience. Ask the Holy Spirit to reveal His heart to you, as He brings to your remembrance all that is needed to usher in healing for your heart.

Do you ever battle with accepting God's will for your life? What kind of fears come up for you? What about it excites you?

_____

_____

_____

_____

_____

_____

Have you ever felt disappointed at where God was leading you? What kind of sacrifices did you have to make? What kind of sacrifices are you making now?

_____

_____

_____

_____

_____

_____

Why do you think it's worth it to surrender your plans for God's plans?

_____
_____
_____
_____
_____
_____
_____

Can you recall a time when you thought where God was taking you seemed harmful but resulted in blessing? Describe it. What was that like for you?

_____
_____
_____
_____
_____
_____
_____
_____
_____

> WE ALL HAVE DREAMS AND DESIRES FOR OUR LIVES. I BELIEVE THAT THERE ARE TIMES WHEN WHAT WE CONSIDER TO BE OUR DREAMS AND DESIRES ARE IN FACT GOD'S.

GOD *of the* IMPOSSIBLE

What are some practical ways you could bring to remembrance all God has done through your trials in the past? How has He kept His promises?

_____
_____
_____
_____
_____
_____

Are you still waiting to understand the purpose behind a decision He made that greatly impacted your life? How are you handling that ambiguity?

_____
_____
_____
_____
_____
_____

Do you invite God into your pain or **DO YOU** ask God to remove your pain? In what ways might God's blessings be made more evident in and through your pain than apart from your pain?

_____
_____
_____

If you were to think about God's will to grow us through pain as His route to promote us, how does that change the way you see your circumstances?

Consider these Scriptures and answer the following questions:

"I am crucified with Christ: nevertheless I live; yet not I, but Christ liveth in me: and the life which I now live in the flesh I live by the faith of the Son of God."
—Galatians 2:20 (KJV)

How do you reconcile the tension between living a life according to your desires and living a life for Christ?

_____
_____
_____
_____
_____
_____

If you have been crucified and now Christ lives in you, what does this say about the power you have to overcome hardship and delight in His will?

_____
_____
_____
_____
_____
_____
_____

"Delight yourself in the Lord, and he will give you the desires of your heart."
—Psalm 37:4

How has this Scripture been taught to you? What do you think David meant by this?

_____
_____

What are the desires of your heart? List your top 3. Do they align with God's will for your life? How could **YOU** affirm this?

Have you ever experienced a change in heart towards the desires you once had? Looking back, why do you think God might have changed your heart?

Write Your Own Prayer

On the lines below, craft your own personal prayer to the Lord. Draw from your answers above as inspiration for the requests you have for God. Ask Him for intimate guidance on what is most important to Him to help you accept and delight in His will, even when it doesn't make sense.

_____
_____
_____
_____
_____
_____
_____
_____
_____
_____
_____
_____
_____
_____
_____
_____
_____
_____
_____
_____

Noted Scriptures

On the lines below, write down a few encouraging Scriptures that you can meditate on, commit to memory, and recite as an expression of hopeful expectation to see God's promises come to pass in your life.

CHAPTER 5

Overcoming Hardships

"These things I have spoken unto you, that in me ye might have peace. In the world ye shall have tribulation: but be of good cheer; I have overcome the world."
—John 16:33 (KJV)

Hardship has a way of tempting us to resign and admit defeat. It pulls at our flesh and whispers in our ears to just give up. Sometimes, we even begin to believe that there's no coming back from a loss so large. Thankfully, we live by a different standard of truth—the truth of the Almighty God Himself, and he whispers a different song: "You've already overcome this because my Son finished the work for you."

> AS WE WALK THROUGH THE VALLEYS, WE ARE UTILIZING FAITH, TRUSTING IN THE UNKNOWN BECAUSE WE KNOW WHO HOLDS OUR TOMORROW.

Questions to Consider:

As you read Chapter 5: "Overcoming Hardships" in *God of the Impossible*, reflect on these questions, wrestle with them, and give yourself room to develop more questions as you journal. Take your time with each one—approach them with intention and patience. Ask the Holy Spirit to reveal His heart to you, as He brings to your remembrance all that is needed to usher in healing for your heart.

Why do you think we are overcomers even when it appears we are losing the battle?

_____
_____
_____
_____
_____
_____
_____

Describe a time when your faith was hanging on by a thread and your heart, thoughts, and actions *did not* align with your identity as an overcomer in Christ. What did you learn from that experience?

_____
_____
_____
_____
_____
_____
_____

Describe a time when your faith was hanging on by a thread, but your heart, thoughts, and actions *did* align with your identity as an overcomer in Christ. What did you learn from that experience?

_____
_____
_____
_____
_____
_____

Drawing from your own experiences, how would you describe God's love and faithfulness as transcending beyond our momentary troubles?

_____
_____
_____
_____
_____
_____

How do you think God fulfills His truth in our lives that we are, in fact, overcomers, in all things?

_____
_____
_____
_____
_____
_____

> **AS CHRISTIANS, WE HAVE BEEN BORN AGAIN, AND IN THIS NEW BIRTH, GOD HAS EQUIPPED US TO BE OVERCOMERS. WE HAVE TO TAKE HOLD OF THAT WHICH HE HAS GIVEN US TO SUCCEED: HIS WORD AND PRAYER.**

Is it possible to be an overcomer without hardship? Who would you be today if you had not endured the fiery furnace?

_____

_____

_____

_____

_____

_____

What kind of differences do you notice take place between when you run to God in your desperation and when you seek distraction or solace in other things?

_____

_____

_____

_____

_____

_____

Why can't we live as victors apart from the Word of God, prayer, and worship? What happens when we fill our minds with His word, pray without ceasing, and worship Him with contrite hearts

_____
_____
_____
_____
_____

How has your faith in your darkest hours impacted another person? How could you begin to think beyond yourself in the middle of your suffering?

_____
_____
_____
_____
_____

Are you diligent in meeting with God face-to-face? How often do you spend alone with Him away from distraction? What are some practical ways you can strengthen this practice? What do you want to see happen as a result?

_____
_____
_____
_____

GOD *of the* **IMPOSSIBLE**

Consider these Scriptures and answer the following questions:

"Do not be afraid or discouraged because of the vast number, for the battle is not yours, but God's."
—2 Chron. 20:15(CSB)

Have you ever seen God fight a battle for you? In what ways did you participate in that fight? What do you think our part is in periods of long-suffering?

How wsell do you give your battles over to God? What are some ways that you try to be self-sufficient? Does that work? Why or why not?

> *"No discipline seems pleasant at the time, but painful. Later on, however, it produces a harvest of righteousness and peace for those who have been trained by it."*
> —Hebrews 12:11 (NIV)

Have you ever found discipline painful? To what degree do you struggle with discipline now? Why do you think that is?

What kind of plan or system can you put in place to exercise the discipline of submitting your life to God daily? What could you improve?

Write Your Own Prayer

On the lines below, craft your own personal prayer to the Lord. Draw from your answers above as inspiration for the requests you have for God. Ask Him for intimate guidance on what is most important to Him to help you overcome what feels like impossible circumstances.

_____
_____
_____
_____
_____
_____
_____
_____
_____
_____
_____
_____
_____
_____
_____
_____
_____
_____
_____
_____

Guided Journal

Noted Scriptures

On the lines below, write down a few encouraging Scriptures that you can meditate on, commit to memory, and recite as an expression of hopeful expectation to see God's promises come to pass in your life.

_____
_____
_____
_____
_____
_____
_____
_____
_____
_____
_____
_____
_____
_____
_____
_____
_____
_____
_____
_____
_____

CHAPTER 6

Lessons in Grief and Pain (Nothing is Wasted)

"He heals the brokenhearted and binds up their wounds."
—Psalm 147:3 (NIV)

God Himself created emotions. Emotions help us build and maintain healthy relationships; they prompt us to take action; they draw us near to Him. God can handle our emotions—the good, the bad, and the ugly. The heart of the Father is FOR US to come before the throne as we are, in every condition—beaten, bruised, and battered—but He does not want us to stay there. He wants to—and WILL—use our worst pain for His glory.

> THE CRUCIAL THING ABOUT GRIEF IS THAT IT MUST BE DEALT WITH, AND REAL LIFE CANNOT START AGAIN UNTIL IT IS.

Questions to Consider:

As you read Chapter 6: "Lessons in Grief and Pain (Nothing is Wasted)" in *God of the Impossible,* reflect on these questions, wrestle with them, and give yourself room to develop more questions as you journal. Take your time with each one—approach them with intention and patience. Ask the Holy Spirit to reveal His heart to you, as He brings to your remembrance all that is needed to usher in healing for your heart.

What has your experience been with the five stages of grief (denial, anger, bargaining, depression, acceptance)? Which stage are you in right now?

_____
_____
_____
_____
_____

What has God placed on your heart that needs healing? Is there something you're avoiding or don't want to face? Why or why not?

_____
_____
_____
_____
_____

What do you think the next step is in your healing? What needs to happen in order for you to get there? Is there anyone in your life who can help you?

_____
_____
_____
_____
_____

Are you harboring any anger, bitterness, resentment, guilt, or shame? Use the lines below to unpack that. Who are you blaming and why? What story could you be telling yourself instead?

_____
_____
_____
_____
_____

What can you thank God for right now? If you are in a season of suffering, where do you see God's hand in it?

_____
_____
_____
_____
_____

Think about events in your life that have produced grief (job loss, divorce, health battle, a dream, etc.). List the events that stand out most strongly in your mind. What aspect of the grieving process looked similar across each event? Different?

_____
_____
_____
_____
_____
_____
_____

What unique lessons about God's heart can you extract from each item on the list above?

_____
_____
_____
_____
_____
_____
_____

Out of the losses you listed, are there any you are still healing from? What kind of practices are you incorporating to complete that healing process?

_____
_____
_____

_____
_____
_____
_____

FINDING MEANING IN DEATH FIRST DEPENDS ON OUR BEING ABLE TO FIND MEANING IN LIFE.

What do you think could be preventing you from moving forward *with* God through your pain? What has prevented you in the past?

_____
_____
_____
_____
_____

How has the purpose and meaning of life for you changed since your most recent or impactful loss?

_____
_____
_____
_____
_____
_____

How is God still good, even when He allows suffering?

_____
_____
_____
_____
_____
_____
_____
_____
_____

How might being still with Him in the messy middle be the best solution until the storm has passed? What do you think God's answer to this question would be?

_____
_____
_____
_____
_____
_____
_____
_____
_____
_____
_____
_____

What has God shown you and taught you in grief? How has he used what appeared to be cruel for good?

_____
_____
_____
_____
_____
_____
_____
_____
_____
_____

Consider these Scriptures and answer the following questions:

> *"All the days ordained for me were written in your book before one of them came to be"*
> —Psalm 139:16 (NIV)

What can you learn about God's sovereignty from this Scripture? What would it be like to worship a god who is unaware of what your future holds?

_____
_____
_____
_____

GOD *of the* **IMPOSSIBLE**

God is not surprised by your pain. How can you take solace in knowing that God has authored your whole life from beginning to end? What does that say about where you find yourself today?

"Every good and perfect gift is from above, coming down from the Father of the heavenly lights"
—James 1:17 (NIV)

How do you typically define God's "gifts"? How do you define what is "good"? How does God define those? How do your definitions and His definitions of each either differ or line up?

What are the good and perfect gifts that God has or is giving you right now? How does it fit into the bigger picture of your past, present, and future?

Write Your Own Prayer

On the lines below, craft your own personal prayer to the Lord. Draw from your answers above as inspiration for the requests you have for God. Ask Him for intimate guidance on what is most important to Him to help you heal and resolve wounds that are hindering His peace from filling your heart and mind.

_____
_____
_____
_____
_____
_____
_____
_____
_____
_____
_____
_____
_____
_____
_____
_____
_____
_____

Guided Journal

Noted Scriptures

On the lines below, write down a few encouraging Scriptures that you can meditate on, commit to memory, and recite as an expression of hopeful expectation to see God's promises come to pass in your life.

_____
_____
_____
_____
_____
_____
_____
_____
_____
_____
_____
_____
_____
_____
_____
_____
_____
_____
_____
_____
_____
_____

CHAPTER 7

Endurance Through the Race of Life

Therefore, since we also have such a large cloud of witnesses surrounding us, let us lay aside every hindrance and the sin that so easily ensnares us. Let us run with endurance the race that lies before us, keeping our eyes on Jesus, the source and perfecter of our faith. For the joy that lay before him, he endured the cross, despising the shame, and sat down at the right hand of the throne of God.
—Hebrews 12:1-2 (CSB)

|||||||||||||||||||||||||||||||||||||||||||||||||||||||

In sports, you enter into the game already an athlete. You have to "have what it takes" in order to make the team and compete. As we work out our own salvation with the Lord, we too need to adopt the mind of an athlete—but our coach takes a different approach to the game called life. He says that we are to come as we are, and He will *make* us into athletes. All we have to do is bring Him a surrendered and obedient heart.

||||||||||||||||||||||||||||||||||||||||||||||||||||||||||||||||||||||||||||||||

GOD CAN ALLOW THINGS TO HAPPEN AND ALLOW THOSE THINGS TO CHANGE US.

||||||||||||||||||||||||||||||||||||||||||||||||||||||||||||||||||||||||||||||||

Questions to Consider:

As you read Chapter 7: "Endurance Through the Race of Life" in *God of the Impossible*, reflect on these questions, wrestle with them, and give yourself room to develop more questions as you journal. Take your time with each one—approach them with intention and patience. Ask the Holy Spirit to reveal His heart to you, as He brings to your remembrance all that is needed to usher in healing for your heart.

What comes to mind when you think of God as your very own personal trainer?

_____

_____

_____

_____

What has God's endurance training for your life looked like?

_____

_____

_____

Guided Journal

_____
_____
_____

What aspects of God's character have you seen or do you see in your own endurance training that stand out to you? What aspects do you want to see more of? How can you begin to ask the Father to reveal them to you?

_____
_____
_____
_____
_____

Do you need to have a competitive or athletic nature in order to embrace endurance training of the spirit? Why or why not?

_____
_____
_____
_____
_____

How is obedience key to finishing the race strong? Where in your life have you observed fatigue as a consequence of disobedience?

_____
_____

GOD *of the* IMPOSSIBLE

_____
_____
_____
_____

||||||||||||||||||||||||||||||||||||||||||||||||||||||||||||||||||||||||||||||||||||

NEVER DOUBT WHOM GOD CAN USE TO ACCOMPLISH HIS PLAN AND PURPOSE IF THEY REMAIN OBEDIENT TO THE DIRECTIONS OF THEIR COACH.

||||||||||||||||||||||||||||||||||||||||||||||||||||||||||||||||||||||||||||||||||||

How can we imitate Jesus when we feel the farthest from Him?
_____
_____
_____
_____
_____

How does the cross help us to reframe the way we see opposition?
_____
_____
_____
_____
_____
_____
_____

Guided Journal

How does God use your disobedience, given repentance, to actually keep you in the race? Have you seen this bear out in your life? What happened?

___

We often wrestle with our faith in times of great upheaval. How do you think God responds to your wrestle? What do you think He sees as He watches you wrestle with trusting Him through it?

___

How is being "hidden" part of God's plan to change you and further His purpose for your life? What can you do in seasons of isolation so that you have the strength to cross the finish line?

___

Consider these Scriptures and answer the following questions:

"The Lord who saved me from the paw of the lion and the paw of the bear will save me from the hand of this Philistine."
—1 Samuel 17:37 (CSB)

Does your faith ever sound like David's in times of sorrow and pain? Why or why not?

_____
_____
_____
_____
_____
_____

When has God saved you from the paw of the lion or the paw of the bear before? How do you think your life would change if these memories were louder than the voice of the enemy as you grieve?

_____
_____
_____
_____
_____
_____
_____

Not that I have already reached the goal or am already perfect, but I make every effort to take hold of it because I also have been taken hold of by Christ Jesus. Brothers and sisters, I do not consider myself to have taken hold of it. But one thing I do: Forgetting what is behind and reaching forward to what is ahead, I pursue as my goal the prize promised by God's heavenly call in Christ Jesus.
—Philippians 3:12-13 (CSB)

In what ways are you dwelling on the past? What do you need to let go of or accept? Why do you think it's so important to let go of the past in order to move toward our future?

_____
_____
_____
_____
_____
_____

Do you believe that healing is taking place right now in your life? In what areas? What can you cling to that will keep you moving forward with hope and assurance of God's great plan for you?

_____
_____
_____
_____
_____
_____
_____

GOD *of the* IMPOSSIBLE

Write Your Own Prayer

On the lines below, craft your own personal prayer to the Lord. Draw from your answers above as inspiration for the requests you have for God. Ask Him for intimate guidance on what is most important to Him to help you finish the grueling race of grieving, receive all that He has to offer, and live in a manner that is worthy of the Lord, no matter what detours you have to take.

_____
_____
_____
_____
_____
_____
_____
_____
_____
_____
_____
_____
_____
_____
_____
_____
_____
_____

Noted Scriptures

On the lines below, write down a few encouraging Scriptures that you can meditate on, commit to memory, and recite as an expression of hopeful expectation to see God's promises come to pass in your life.

_____
_____
_____
_____
_____
_____
_____
_____
_____
_____
_____
_____
_____
_____
_____
_____
_____
_____
_____
_____
_____
_____
_____
_____

> **AS WE RUN THE RACE IN OUR OWN LANES, WE COME TO REALIZE THAT WE ARE GROWING IN FAITH AND INTIMACY WITH GOD THE FATHER, GOD THE SON, AND GOD THE HOLY SPIRIT.**

As you finish this companion journal, may your lives be changed, may it help you encounter God, and may it empower you to be led by the Holy Spirit, our companion and guide Who always points us to a personal relationship and daily walk with Jesus our Savior, friend, and soon-coming King!

www.ingramcontent.com/pod-product-compliance
Lightning Source LLC
Chambersburg PA
CBHW062120080426
42734CB00012B/2933